The 4th Dimension Absolute Positivity Training School

Absolute Positivity Training School Series 1

The 4th Dimension Absolute Positivity Training School

Younghoon Lee

POSITIVITY

CGW | LOGOS USA

| Prologue |

Positivity wins everything. God's absolute positive love changes everything. Originally, humans were beings of absolute despair and absolute negativity. However, God changed absolute despair into absolute hope and absolute negativity into absolute positivity through Jesus' cross. When Jesus came into this world that was full of sin, death, despair, solitude, and sadness, all the injustice that had been in our lives disappeared.

As Christians, we who have been a slave to sin are now a child of God. We have been transformed into people who speak anew, dream anew, and act anew in the cross. However, there are still many times when we can't get out of the thoughts, words, and habits of our old self. There are many times when we have negative thoughts, words, and actions. This is why we need training for new habits of absolute positivity.

To help with this training, we created a textbook called 4th Dimension Absolute Positivity Training School. In each lecture, we measure our positive index and engage in a lecture topic and have a time for small group sharing. Each lecture also contains a rich Bible verse to meditate on, providing an opportunity to train for positivity according to biblical principles. We'll learn about having a positive view of self, others, work, environment, and the future. Through positive training, we use positive language, absolute gratitude, and sharing love, to be charged with positive energy in life.

I recommend that you form a group either at home, in a cell district or in a small group, in a church or institution, and use it as a training textbook. If you refer to *The Miracle of Absolute Positivity*, which I wrote together, you will be able to have a greater overall experience. The God of absolute positivity is planning and preparing amazing things for your life. Have hope and look forward to the good things that all of you will experience, through the miracle of absolute positivity and this textbook.

Rev. Dr. **Younghoon Lee**
Senior Pastor of Yoido Full Gospel Church

How to use the textbook

1. Learning objectives

1) Meditate and internalize words related to absolute positivity according to biblical principles.
2) Realize the importance of absolute positive attitude and faith. You are transformed into an absolute positive person by learning and training through the Fivefold positivity and Threefold training.
3) Try to make the habit of absolute positivity in your daily life.
4) Study with small group members, gather absolute positive energy and positive vibes to create a positive community.
5) Change into an absolute positive person to live a balanced faith life and become a spiritually successful person who achieves God's dream and mission.

2. Content composition

The 4th Dimension Absolute Positivity Training School consists of seven parts for each chapter.

1 — Introductory example and meditation

2 — PQ (Positive Index) Check List

3 — Encounter the Word

4 — Lecture on topic

5 — Absolutely positive hymn

6 — Small group workshop

7 — Proclamation of gratitude

How to use the textbook

Absolute Positivity Diagram

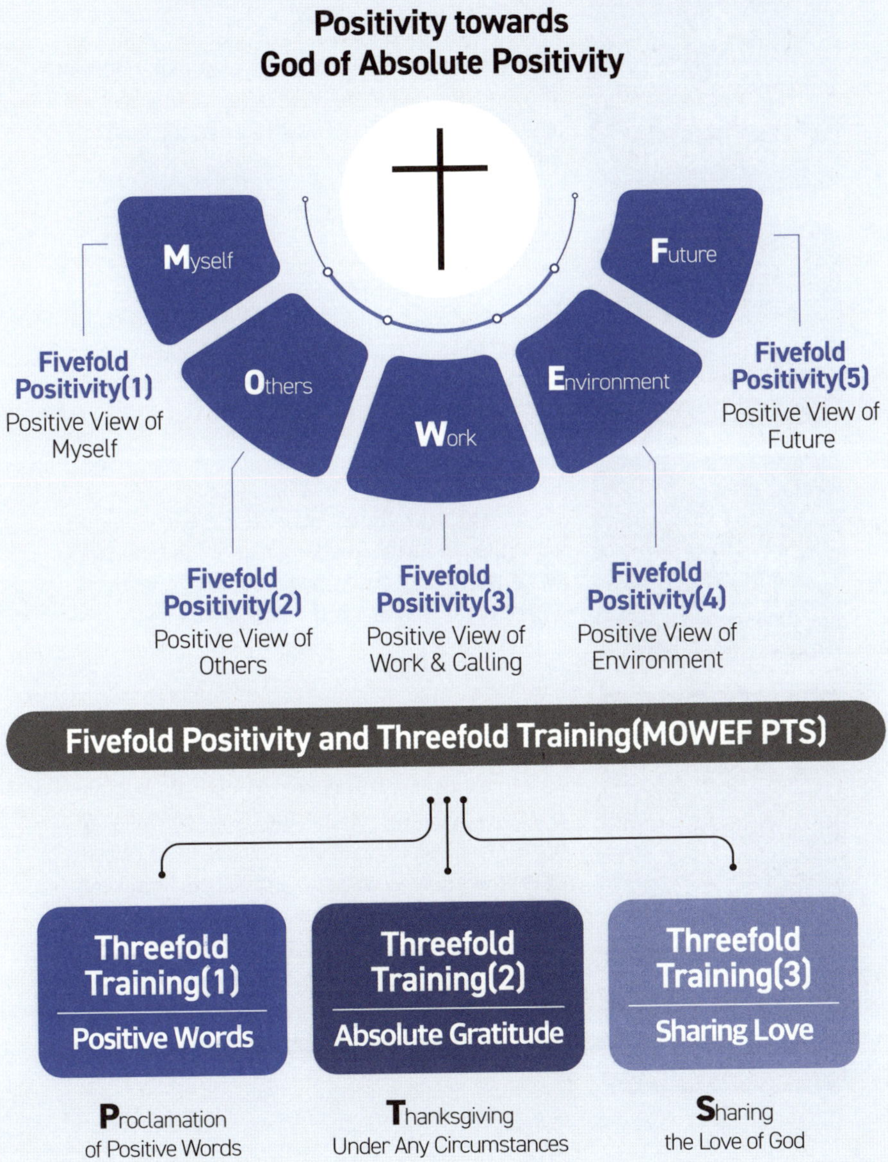

How to use the textbook

3. How to use it

① Introductory example and meditation	Read and meditate on the introductory example. Share thoughts, feelings, and past experiences through the example. And after a moment of meditation, share what was learned through the meditation.
② PQ (Positive Index) Checklist	Evaluate your positive index by checking honestly. Add up the scores for each of the 10 questions.
③ Encounter the Word	It's time to study the Bible related to each topic of absolute positivity. Read the text of the Bible and write down the answers to the five questions. Share what was learned through that text.
④ Lecture on topic	Study the subject of the lecture related to absolute positivity. The importance of absolute positivity, positive about the God of absolute positivity, Fivefold positivity: positive view of self, others, work, environment, and future. Study and apply the training of positive language, absolute gratitude, and sharing love. Look for the rich Bible verse in each paragraph and study meditatingly. Share thoughts, experiences, visions, and so on that are relevant to each topic and phrase.

How to use the textbook

⑤ Absolutely positive hymn

It's time to think about the topic and what was learned in the chapter. Sing a praise of positivity. Pray earnestly and praise together, seeking the presence and help of the Holy Spirit.

⑥ Small group workshop

It's time to divide what was learned about absolute positivity in small groups. It is important to share feelings and resolutions with the members through each lecture and look at them with faith. Block negative thoughts and words and encourage each other to have positive habits. Let's faithfully carry out the assignment and check it next time.

⑦ Proclamation of gratitude

God's word is always positive. Recite every week the words associated with absolute positivity. Summarize and declare the topics learned in each chapter, declare them as faith to yourself and to each other. Let's all say the Proclamation out loud together. Meditate on the wise words of positivity and summarize what was learned that day and take notes.

Everyone who practices and learns according to this textbook will be transformed into an absolute positive person. Raising the absolute Positive Index PQ will be the biggest asset in your life. I hope that God's special grace and wisdom will overflow to those who begin this study. Let's fill out the 4th Dimension Absolute Positivity Training School admission pledge and begin a journey of learning.

Admission Pledge

As a trainee of the 4th Dimension Absolute Positivity Training School, I pledge before God, as follows.

1. I will try my best not to have any negative thoughts or words during the 4th Dimension Absolute Positivity Training School.
2. I will faithfully participate in the 4th Dimension Absolute Positivity Training School without being absent or tardy.
3. I will honestly fill out the positive index PQ checklist and evaluate myself with candidness.
4. I will sincerely study and meditate on the Bible verses of absolute positivity learning in the textbook.
5. I will faithfully carry out the assignments and memorize the Bible verses.
6. I will encourage my classmates who are learning together with me by creating a positive community with positive energy.
7. Through this school, I will try to raise my positive index PQ and become an absolute positive person with a dream.

Date: _____ / _____ / _______(MM/DD/YYYY)

Name: Signature:

Contents

POSITIVITY

01

The Importance of Absolute Positivity

01 The Importance of Absolute Positivity

In America, a certain Christian man had spent a lifetime filled with failures and despair rather than happiness. His business venture failed at age 22, he failed in the state elections at age 23, he failed again in business at age 24. He was elected to state legislature at 25, the woman he loved died when he was 26. At age 27, he had a nervous breakdown and schizophrenia, he ran for Congress at 29, lost the presidency at 31, lost the House of Representatives at 34, at age 37 he was barely elected as a Representative to lose it 2 years later. That wasn't the end, at age 46 he lost the Senate race, at age 47 he lost the bid for Vice Presidency, and at the age of 49 he lost the Senate race again. Then, at the age of 51, he was elected the 16th President of the United States.

His name is Abraham Lincoln. He became God's great servant who laid a great foundation for the establishment of true human rights and peace in America. He ended slavery and created the possibility of civil and social freedom for African Americans. His life seemed to be a series of failures and discouragements, however, without despair he moved forward with the faith of absolute positivity. God accomplished many great things through him.

Meditation

What kind of failures have I experienced in my life so far?
What did I learn from the process?

Positivity Quotient Check List

Positive Attitude Quotient Check List?

Instructions: Please read each statement and select the most appropriate response to indicate how frequently you experience the behavior described in the statement.

Statements	Never	Rarely	Some times	Often	Always
	1	2	3	4	5
1. When stressed, I think positively and overcome it.					
2. Negative emotions don't determine the attitude or direction of life.					
3. After experiencing hardship and difficulty, I learn from them and get back up.					
4. I usually believe in the power of positivity and am very conscious about it.					
5. I have high expectations of my remaining life and future.					
6. When looking at the environment or people, I try to see the brighter side than the darker.					
7. I visualize myself doing well or succeeding.					
8. There are more people who say positive things around me than negative things.					
9. I don't think I'm going to fail at something before I start it.					
10. I have a lot of love and positive energy in me.					

After reading each statement, check the corresponding box.
Add up the checked scores for each statement.

Totals (   ) points

Encounter the Word

Read Jeremiah 29:10-13.

10 *This is what the LORD says: "When seventy years are completed for*
Babylon, I will come to you and fulfill my good promise to bring you
back to this place. 11 *For I know the plans I have for you," declares the*
LORD, "plans to prosper you and not to harm you, plans to give you
hope and a future. 12 *Then you will call on me and come and pray to*
me, and I will listen to you. 13 *You will seek me and find me when you*
seek me with all your heart.

1. What prophetic message is God giving to the people of Israel who are in despair as they have been taken as prisoners to Babylon? (Verse 10)

2. What is God's plan for us? Why did he say that "I know" here? (Verse 11)

3. What is the way to know God's thoughts and plans and be hopeful when you are discouraged or in despair? (Verse 12)

4. What attitude should you have when you go before the Lord? (Verse 13)

5. God wants us to have an absolute positive hope even in a situation of absolute despair. What is the reason? (cf. Jeremiah 29:11; John 3:16; Isaiah 61:3)

The Importance of Absolute Positivity

One of the most important things in life is to create a positive image of yourself. Life becomes the reality of what we think and visualize. Why is absolute positivity important in our lives?

1. Positive people are healthy

It has been said that negative thoughts and stresses are linked to mental and physical illnesses. A happy heart makes the face cheerful, but heartache crushes the spirit(Proverbs 15:13). A cheerful heart is good medicine for our body and mind(Proverbs 17:22). Peace and joy of the mind are more likely to appear in people with positive thoughts and attitudes.

Dr. Emerson of the U.S. National Health Service conducted an experiment to find out the relationship between gratitude and health. Through this study, he has concluded that the frequent use of positive language and words of gratitude increases immunity, helping to overcome large and small diseases and living a much healthier life.

Q What should we do to protect and guard our heart? (Proverbs 4:23)

2. People with positive attitudes are happier

People with positive attitudes are happier. Two psychologists have conducted an experiment analyzing 141 yearbook photos of Mills College from the graduating class of 1960. They followed up with the lives of the graduates. Compared to the people who were expressionless on the graduation photos, those who genuinely smiled called Duchenne, showed a high sense of accomplishment, a good interpersonal relationship, a stable psychological state, and a high level of personal income.

Sonja Lyubomirsky, a psychology professor in America who had been doing research on Positive Psychology says, "What brings happiness is a positive attitude to life." Even the Apostle Paul, when imprisoned urged us to be "Always be joyful."(Philippians 4:4) Our mind is what really matters the most, even more than our circumstance.

Q

What should we do to eat good things and enjoy our lives? (Isaiah 55:2)

3. People with positive attitudes are more successful

Life is a battle between positivity and negativity. The human mind is a battlefield of positivity and negativity. For healthier sustainable success, you must work through visualization of positive images. Many successful businessmen and famous athletes know the importance of visualization and image training and practice.

Conformity is the energy that causes waves to react to other objects. Human emotions can also have a similar phenomenon. The same goes for positive energy(cf. Proverbs 27:17).

So, if you want to be successful in what you're doing, you must surround yourself with people with positive energy. I should be the one that sends out positive energy and influences others to come together as a positive community.

> **Q** What kind of image do you have about yourself, about others, about work? And what image do you have of your church, company, community, and of the problem(s)? A positive or negative picture? (cf. Hebrews 11:1)

4. A positive person is highly resilient

Resilience is when an individual or community that has experienced adversity or unhappiness has the power to recover and find its place or climb higher without being discouraged. A positive person is highly resilient and can overcome any hardships in life.

According to Professor Emmy E. Werner, there are three factors to resilience: self-regulation, interpersonal skills, and positivity. The most important among those three is positivity. Strengthening positivity can increase self-regulation and interpersonal skills at the same time, and when it becomes a habit, it can increase resilience for any individual.

A positive person can turn an obstacle into a steppingstone(cf. Judges

3:12-31). A person's attitude towards hardships in life can tell much about ones positivity. A negative person can stumble over the smallest of things. A positive person can fulfill God's dream by sublimating any hardships in life(Psalm 119:71).

Q	What attitude does the Apostle Peter recommend us to take when tests or concerns approach us? (1 Peter 1:6; 1 Peter 3:14; 1 Peter 4:12-13; 1 Peter 5:7)

5. Increase your Positivity Quotient, PQ

Just as each person has an Intelligence Quotient IQ different from their Emotional Quotient EQ, the Positive Quotient PQ is also different. Go through Absolute Positivity Quotient Check Lists at the end of each chapter of this guidebook. Evaluate your positive index/quotient using the PQ measurement prepared. May your PQ increase through the practice and guide questions. A higher individual's PQ will lead to meaningful transformations in life and faith, and a higher community's PQ will help the community to renew and to fulfill their higher callings. May all of you be the heroes of miracles of absolute positivity.

Draw Me Nearer

W.H.Donae

Commitment and Application

1. Let's share about moments of God's grace you experienced this past week.

2. We have studied about the "Importance of Absolute Positivity." Let's share what we felt and realized today.

3. How am I managing my thought for my health?

4. Am I happy now? How happy am I? If not, let's share what the reasons are.

5. Let's share about what our expectations are of *The 4th Dimension Absolute Positivity Training School.*

Today's Assignment	Have you had any problems or concerns recently? Let's think about the positive results and write them down.

Memory Verses

"Above all else, guard your heart,
for everything you do flows from it."
Proverbs 4:23

Proclamation of Absolute Positivity

"I know the value and importance of
absolute positivity and will devote myself
to raising the positivity index!"

Meditation Quote

"It is an outward look on our past experiences.
It is the prophet of our future."
John Maxwell

POSITIVITY

02

Positivity towards God of Absolute Positivity

02 Positivity towards God of Absolute Positivity

A young man in Ireland met tragedy of his beloved fiancée drowning a day before their wedding. The young man went to Canada to avoid memories and the surroundings reminding him of the pain but before he could settle down, he heard that his mother back in his hometown was seriously ill and awaiting her last moment. Every misfortune in the world seemed to come his way like a tornado. The young man knelt helplessly before God and sobbed. "Jesus, please heal my mother's illness. I will live for your glory for the rest of my life."

In that moment, God's comfort and peace came into his heart. He sent a letter to his mom who was bedridden, and soon he received good news in return of her complete recovery. This young man's name is Joseph M. Scriven.

His prayer of absolute positivity amid the deepest despair brought the miracle of his mother's healing. He was inspired to write during his prayer time becoming the lyrics of Hymn 369, "What a friend we have in Jesus". The second verse goes like this, Have we trials and temptations" is there troubles anywhere we should never be discouraged. Take it to the Lord in prayer!"

Meditation

When you pray with faith of absolute positivity, doors will be opened(Matthew 7:7).
Let's think about how to pray and receive breakthrough if your path is currently blocked.

Positivity Quotient Check List ☑

Positive Faith Quotient Check List?

Instructions: Please read each statement and select the most appropriate response to indicate how frequently you experience the behavior described in the statement.

Statements	Never	Rarely	Some times	Often	Always
	1	2	3	4	5
1. God is the most important person in my life and I believe I love Him the most.					
2. I believe God is with me when I pray.					
3. I believe the cross of Jesus Christ displays the love of God's absolute positivity.					
4. No matter what hardship and difficulty, I am not discouraged because God is present.					
5. I engage with God and talk to Him daily.					
6. When what I want isn't quickly achieved, I think and wait, "There will be God's timing."					
7. In my faith life, I experience and am greatly moved by God's love.					
8. When I pray, I often experience despair and negative thoughts disappearing.					
9. I read and meditate on God's Word daily.					
10. I believe that whether you're good, evil, at peace or struggling, it's all under God's sovereignty.					

After reading each statement, check the corresponding box.
Add up the checked scores for each statement.

Totals (   ) points

Encounter the Word

Read through Hebrews 11:1-3 and 11:6.

1 *Now faith is confidence in what we hope for and assurance about what we do not see.* 2 *This is what the ancients were commended for.* 3 *By faith we understand that the universe was formed at God's command, so that what is seen was not made out of what was visible…*
6 *And without faith it is impossible to please God, because anyone who comes to him must believe that he exists and that he rewards those who earnestly seek him.*

1. How does today's text define faith? (Verse 1)
   What can we learn from the definition of faith?

2. What does it say the universe was formed with? (Verse 3)

3. What does "what is seen was not made out of what was visible" mean in verse 3?
   Meditate on it in relation to 4th Dimension Spirituality.
   (cf. Yonggi Cho, 4th Dimension Spirituality, Church Growth Institute, 2010)

4. What pleases our Lord? (Verse 6a) How am I pleasing the Lord?

5. What must we believe when we come before the Lord? (Verse 6b)

Positivity towards God of Absolute Positivity

At the center and beginning of all positivity is God, who is positive. In this session, we'll find out who God is in the Bible and why it's so important to have faith of absolute positivity in God.

1. God of Absolute Positivity

Our Lord is the God of Absolute Positivity. When God created the world, He said it was well(Genesis 1:31). God so loved the world even after man's fall(John 3:16), God planned the salvation of the mankind through Jesus(Ephesians 1:4), Christian faith is absolute positivity. The cross of Jesus Christ is at the center of it.

There is no negativity in the gospel. The gospel of the cross is complete and full. It is a message of God's absolute positivity. Our faithful and gracious God wants our body, soul, and spirit to be well(3 John 1:2). When you believe in Jesus Christ, you receive eternity, fullness of the Holy Spirit, healing of your body and spirit, all peace will be with us and when Jesus returns, we enter into Heaven with Him. Thus, the gospel is good news of a great joy(Luke 2:10).

Q The Bible tells us to "Taste and see that the Lord is good"(Psalm 34:8). Has your faith ever been shaken in the faith of God's goodness?

2. The Sovereign love of God

Jesus is the main character of the Bible and the main theme is the love of God(John 3:16; 1 John 4:19). When we realize the abundant immense love of God towards us, we can trust in the Lord with our faith of absolute positivity. The Bible tells us that God works for the good of those who love him, who have been called according to his purpose(Romans 8:28). It is hard to expect anything positive in mankind who are tainted with sin. But the cross of Jesus Christ has transformed all the negativity to positivity. Those who trust in the sovereignty of the Lord and his complete control in our lives, can come forward with the faith of absolute positivity(Hebrews 11:6).

God has called us before time began and made us his children. "Do not fear, for I have redeemed you; I have summoned you by name; you are mine."(Isaiah 43:1)

Reverend Yonggi Cho always emphasized the love of God in absolute positivity which was the main theme of this book, "4th Dimension Spirituality."(Thoughts of God, Faith of God, Dream of God, and Words of God)

Q When and how did you realize God's personal love for you? (cf. Isaiah 43:1) Reflect on it and share your experience with others.

3. God who shines light amidst the darkness

There's a mosaic making art game. Mosaic play requires both bright and dark colored paper. A beautiful work is created only when bright and dark colors are used and arranged well. The same goes for our lives. Not only joy and pride, but also sorrow, pain, and hardship are combined to create a wonderful picture of life. Therefore, in the midst of hardship and darkness, we must seek to find God's truth, love, and light(Isaiah 45:7). We must not lose faith of absolute positivity.

Satan killed the son of God through Governor Pilate and Jewish leaders, but God made this a way of salvation for all. For Joseph, a man of dreams and faith, endured the 13 years of hardship knowing it wasn't a failure, but a way to save himself and save the nation. Joseph confessed God's sovereignty and the providence of love to his brothers who betrayed and sold him(Genesis 50:20).

Job, a righteous man in the East, suffered from the loss of all his property, family, and even his health. However, Job was blessed twice as much with his faith in God in the end. Even in all these trials he did not complain nor resent God but trusted in the Lord of absolute positivity(Job 1:22; Job 42:10).

Q What must we remember when trials and despair come our way? (Isaiah 45:7)

4. Faith of absolute positivity that brings miracles

We must believe that our God is the God of goodness, faithfulness and love. No matter how hard our lives may be, when we have faith of absolute positivity, we will experience that God works all things together for the good of us. God wants to give us hope and a future. He wants to bless us(Jeremiah 29:11). We must remember that "Nothing is taken away from us when we pray. We don't lose when we pray." God always has the best interest and plan for us. He will work through the best way at the right time.

We must believe that our God is faithful(2 Corinthians 1:18). God never disappoint those who faithfully trust him. He makes a way where there is none. He opens closed doors. All that we can't do, He is able to do beyond measure. When we pray with faith of absolute positivity while we wait and anticipate, miracles will certainly occur.

Q What attitude did King Hezekiah have when he was faced with death? How did the Lord answer his prayer? (Isaiah 38:1-8)

Those Who Love the Lord

Younghoon Lee

Commitment and Application

1. Share about God's grace you have experienced this past week.

2. We have studied together on "Positivitiy towards God of Absolute Positivity." Share what you have learned from it.

3. Meditate on the statement. What does it mean? Share with one another. "Jesus changed all negativity to positivity."

4. Why must we not fall into despair nor be dismayed when trials and hardships come? Why must we have faith of absolute positivity? (Romans 8:28)

5. Recall a time when you prayed with faith of absolute positivity. Share.

Today's Assignment

Choose 3 people from the Bible who possessed absolute positive faith and summarize what they did to follow through.

Memory Verses

"We know that in all things
God works for the good of those who love him,
who have been called according to his purpose."
Romans 8:28

Proclamation of Absolute Positivity

" I believe that
God is the God of absolute positivity
And trust God completely!"

Meditation Quote

"Never say the word impossible
Just throw it away in the trash."
Goethe

POSITIVELY

03

Fivefold Positivity ①: Positive View of Myself

03 Fivefold Positivity ①: Positive View of Myself

There was a beggar who was kindhearted and had no greed. One day, God came to him and asked, "I will grant your three wishes, so tell me anything you want."

"The beggar pondered for a long time, and as his first wish, he asked for an aluminum can for rice and side dishes. The beggar said his second wish was to have a stainless steel can stronger than an aluminum can. God said, "Now what is your last wish? I will grant you anything you want so ask me anything." After deep consideration, the beggar then said, "God, this is my last wish. Please allow me to have a thermos rice container." He needed a rice container to keep the food warm that he got from begging.

Why did this beggar only ask of these little things? Perhaps, it is because of his self-perception. He had a chance of asking the Almighty God for anything but what he asked was so limited to his own idea of asking for a cool can. A positive future may begin with a positive self-perspective and positive thoughts. The Apostle Paul said, "To him who is able to do far more abundantly beyond all that we ask or think, according to the power that works within us."(Ephesians 3:20)

Meditation Let's think about our self-image and how it affects our prayer.

Positivity Quotient Check List

Positive View of Myself Quotient Check List?

Instructions: Please read each statement and select the most appropriate response to indicate how frequently you experience the behavior described in the statement.

Statements	Never	Rarely	Some times	Often	Always
	1	2	3	4	5
1. I think I'm attractive.					
2. I don't compare myself with others and feel inferior.					
3. I believe that God made me unique and precious.					
4. I think I have enough qualifications to be loved.					
5. I feel happy now.					
6. I am not swayed by people's gossip or criticism.					
7. I believe that I have talent and value.					
8. I value and love myself.					
9. I think I can do well with whatever I'm entrusted with.					
10. I picture my future self as I declare and bless my future.					

After reading each statement, check the corresponding box.
Add up the checked scores for each statement.

Totals (   ) points

Encounter the Word

Read Psalm 139:14-18.

14 *I praise you because I am fearfully and wonderfully made; your*
works are wonderful, I know that full well. 15 *My frame was not*
hidden from you when I was made in the secret place, when I was
woven together in the depths of the earth. 16 *Your eyes saw my*
unformed body; all the days ordained for me were written in your
book before one of them came to be. 17 *How precious to me are your*
thoughts, God! How vast is the sum of them! 18 *Were I to count them,*
they would outnumber the grains of sand—when I awake, I am still
with you.

1. What does today's scripture say about God's creation of us? (Verse 14)

2. What is the meaning of "My frame was not hidden?" (Verse 15) (Job 34:21; Psalm 7:9)

3. What are the Lord's thoughts about me? (Verse 17) What is the meaning of "They would outnumber the grains of sand?" (Verse 18)

4. We must live according to the Lord's calling. Where does it say that our days are written in? (Verse 16) What does this verse this mean? (Psalm 90:12)

5. Lev Tolstoy said, "What men live by is love not bread" This is the real spiritual food that we need. (cf. Isaiah 49:15-16; Matthew 4:4)

Fivefold Positivity ①: Positive View of Myself

With positive thoughts in mind, we must guard our hearts(Proverbs 4:23). The most important way to guard our heart is to have positive thoughts of ourselves. When the foundation is shaken, all things in life may collapse with it.

1. The Importance of Positive Self-Image and Self-Esteem

1) Positive self-image and self-esteem and life's happiness

The enemy's attacks on our self-worth is relentless, giving us negative thoughts and low self-esteem, constantly instilling feelings of depression, fear, anger, comparison and inferiority in our mind. People with low self-esteem are likely to be addicted to things that give pleasure and they may have a more difficult time in being satisfied and happy. Happiness doesn't come when you compare yourself to others(cf. 2 Corinthians 10:12) but rather, when you live according to the life that the Lord has ordained for you. Let's meditate on the talents and gifts that the Lord has given us. Let's give thanks to Him.

2) Positive self-image and self-esteem and successful interpersonal relationship

When you have a positive self-perception and can love yourself, you can have successful interpersonal relationships. When you are unable to see yourself through the lens of love, you may not be able to see others through the lens of love. A person who cannot see themselves with a lens of love cannot see anyone else with a lens of love. If you consider yourself insignificant, others will feel it and treat you as insignificant(Ephesians 5:28). If you are positive and love yourself, you'll have the respect and honor of others.

3) Positive view of self and love for others

Those who are positive about themselves can live a life that fulfills God's purpose and mission. Self-perception determines the level of his or her thoughts and prayers. When you are filled with the Holy Spirit, you realize your precious value and mission and God's vision and dreams(Joel 2:28).

Q Let's write down five strengths and share with one another.

2. Positive self-perception strategies

1) Remember that I am God's masterpiece

For you to have a positive self-perception, you must realize that you are God's masterpiece. Any work made by a famous composer or painter becomes a masterpiece. Each one of us is a masterpiece of God just because God Almighty the Creator made it himself(Psalm 139:14). There is only one person in human history who is "You" You must realize your value, respect yourself, and look at yourself as God's beloved.

Q The Bible tells us that we are blessed, why is that? (Deuteronomy 33:29)

2) A new self-image gained through the lens of the cross

We can realize two important truths through the cross. First, we can see the price of our sins. Our sins were so enormous and heavy that God had to allow his son Jesus to die for us(Romans 3:23). Second, you can see the value of God's love. God loved us to the extent that He willingly gave up his son(Galatians 2:20). The cross shows how great the sin of man is and how great the love of God is at the same time. Therefore, I must feel the great love of God the Father through the lens of the cross and increase my self-esteem(Isaiah 49:15-16).

Q What does the Bible tell us of our existence? (1 Peter 2:9)

---

3) Acknowledge your weakness, Give them to the Lord

Positive self-perception and self-centeredness should not be confused. Self-centeredness is the result of a negative self-image, not positive self-perception. Complete positive self-perception begins with acknowledgement of our weaknesses. Those who know how small we are can humble themselves before the Lord and depend on Him wholeheartedly(2 Chronicles 33:12; 1 Peters 5:5).

Absolute positivity towards God strengthens us and gives us courage, confidence, and visions. Regardless of our weaknesses, flaws, and circumstances, we must come to the Lord with the faith of absolute positivity and have a positive self-perception. This way, all that was ordained for us will come to fulfillment.

Q What sin does Moses, David and Paul have in common? (Exodus 2:12; 2 Samuel 11:15; Acts 7:58) and what are the hidden spiritual lessons behind them?

4) Bless yourself with self-fulfilling prophecy

Good prophecy refers to speaking and proclaiming God's thoughts and words with the heart of God's love(Jeremiah 2:1, 1 Corinthians 14:1, 3) and it must be first applied to oneself. God said to Abraham, "You will be a blessing."(Genesis 12:2) Today, the same is for us as descendants of Abraham's faith. When we believed in Jesus, we were already blessed(Galatians 3:14).

When you know the love that God has for you, you can bless yourself with self-fulfilling prophecy. Look in the mirror and bless yourself by including your name.

"Hey, you've already become a source of blessing. Many will be blessed by heaven and earth through you!"

Q Let's try blessing ourselves, how would you like to bless yourself?

The Trusting Heart to Jesus Clings

W. J. Kirkpatrick

Commitment and Application

1. Let's share the moments where you experienced God's grace this past week.

2. We have studied about "Positivity View of Myself."
   Let's share what we felt and realized today.

3. What stood out to you from the reasons why positive self-perception is important?

4. Why do you think is most important to have a positive self-perception?

5. Let's share about our strengths and gifts and God's calling and vision behind them.

Today's Assignment

Write a self-fulfilling prophecy of yourself as you bless your present and future.

Memory Verses

"Everyone who is called by my name,
whom I created for my glory,
Whom I formed and made."
Isaiah 43:7

Proclamation of Absolute Positivity

"I am the Lord's masterpiece and
I believe that He will bless me
and use me according to His will!"

Meditation Quote

"If you are positive,
you'll see opportunities instead of obstacles."
Widad Akrawi

POSITIVITY

04

Fivefold Positivity ②: Positive View of Others

04 Fivefold Positivity ②: Positive View of Others

Every year on April 15th, all American Major League Baseball players play games with the number 42 on their back. It is to commemorate Jacky Robinson, the first African American baseball player. He was the first African American player to receive the Rookie of the year award in 1947. He also won the National League's Most Valuable Player Award(MVP) in 1949. He was inducted into the Baseball Hall of Fame in 1962.

As a baseball player, he experienced discrimination and ridicule because white supremacy was prevalent at that time. One day, he made a defensive error. The crowd booed, and even the fellow players did not hide their abusive language and unpleasant expressions. At the height of the gruesome atmosphere, Harold Peter Henry Reese also known as "Pee Wee" Reese, was in the shortstop position. He approached Jackie Robinson, took off his glove and hugged him. The two laughed and talked. The atmosphere of the stadium changed instantly. Jackie Robinson said at that time that he was reborn. Without the encouragement of Harold Peter Henry Reese, perhaps the legendary player would not have existed.

With a genuine smile, kind words, mindful encouragements and helping hands, God's love in us will be shared to those around us.

Meditation

As we encounter people, do we look at them with God's eyes and treat them kindly?

Positivity Quotient Check List

Positive View of Others Quotient Check List?

Instructions: Please read each statement and select the most appropriate response to indicate how frequently you experience the behavior described in the statement.

Statements	Never	Rarely	Some times	Often	Always
	1	2	3	4	5
1. When I see others, I try to see their strengths than their weaknesses.					
2. It isn't difficult to talk with someone who thinks differently than me.					
3. I'm happy to help someone in a difficult situation.					
4. I consider other people's feelings and value them.					
5. When treating others, I don't lose my smile and friendliness.					
6. I cherish the people I meet and bless them.					
7. If it's for someone else, I can take a loss.					
8. I can be friendly to people who misunderstand and hate me.					
9. I tend to encourage and praise people.					
10. I can forgive the person who hurt me or gave me a difficult time.					

After reading each statement, check the corresponding box.
Add up the checked scores for each statement.

Totals (   ) points

Encounter the Word

Read Matthew 20:25-28.

25 *Jesus called them together and said, "You know that the rulers of the Gentiles lord it over them, and their high officials exercise authority over them.* 26 *Not so with you. Instead, whoever wants to become great among you must be your servant,* 27 *and whoever wants to be first must be your slave—* 28 *just as the Son of Man did not come to be served, but to serve, and to give his life as a ransom for many."*

1. How does Jesus say that powerful people in the world are to treat others? (Verse 25)

2. How should Jesus' disciples treat one another, children of God? (Verses 26-27)

3. Why did Jesus come to this earth? (Verse 28)

4. What is the difference between world leadership and spiritual leadership? (Verses 25-27)

5. Let's meditate and share what the meaning of 'serving others' in the text means.

Positive View of Others

When you meet the God of absolute positivity, not only do your thoughts about yourself change but thoughts of others change as well. We look at others with God's eyes, becoming God's ears, we listen to others, becoming God's hands, we wipe away the tears of others, becoming God's feet, we walk with the lonely, and convey God's love to others.

1. The Importance of having a positive perspective of others

1) It's the proof of God's love

The Bible says that it is impossible to love God and not love your neighbor or brother(1 John 4:7-8; Galatians 5:14). You cannot hate the people he loves and say that you love God(John 3:16). God's love is the reason for the love of our neighbor, and our neighbor's love is the fruit of God's love.

2) Become a channel of blessing

God said to Abraham, "You will be a blessing...All the peoples on earth will be blessed through you."(Genesis 12:2-3) He gave the word of promise. This is because he wanted all the peoples of the earth to be blessed with knowing God through Abraham. The word God gave to Abraham applies to us today. When I become a channel of blessing with faith, God's grace and love will flow to the people around me, my church, my nation and the nations throughout the world.

3) I myself benefit as well

American psychologist Adam Grant says, "Giver" is more likely to succeed than the "Taker" who takes more than they're given." The "Matcher" gives as much as they've received." A person who brings out the person's success succeeds, as the probability of success for the people around them increases(cf. Acts 20:35). Kindness and consideration make very important contributions to successful interpersonal relationships.

Consideration and kindness makes a relationship better, making myself and the other person successful. Having a positive perspective of others and helping them succeed is the secret to our success(cf. Luke 6:38).

Q

The Apostle Paul said, "To respect one another first."(Romans 12:10) Let's meditate on what is said and share what it means.

2. Ways of having a positive perspective of others

1) Speak positive words

Relationship expert Dr. John Gottman said that happy couples use positive words at least five times more than negative words. This is called Gottman's 5:1 Ratio. When dealing with others, it's important to say a lot of positive things, as well as being considerate, encouraging, and praising(Proverbs 27:21). American politician Benjamin Franklin said, "The secret to success lies in revealing the merits of the other person without gossiping." Words of positivity lead us to successful interpersonal relationships.

Q

How do positive words of encouragement affect you physically and emotionally? (Proverbs 16:24)

2) Speak words of blessing

God is the source of all blessings(Genesis 1:28), but that blessing all originates from man's word of mouth(Numbers 6:27; 2 Chronicles 30:27), God has blessed us as a royal priesthood and has given us the power to bless(Numbers 23:20; Psalm 118:26), so when we speak words of curses it brings us harm as well(Psalm 109:18). Therefore, we must bless our families and children(2 Samuel 6:20; Genesis 49:28), bless our superiors and authorities(1 Kings 1:47) and non-believers as well(Genesis 47:10). Moreover, we must be able to bless those who persecute us(Romans 12:14), our food(Mark 8:7) and what our future holds as well(Hebrews 11:20). Until we go see the Lord, we have the holy calling of blessing everything and everyone around us(Deuteronomy 33:1).

Q

What does the Apostle Paul say he will bring to the saints in the church of Rome? (Romans 15:29)

3) Be kind

Kindness, which also means to show mercy, is one of the nine fruit of the Holy Spirit (Galatians 5:22-23). There is a saying in Talmud that says, "be kind to strangers, you may be entertaining angels."(cf. Hebrews 13:2; Genesis 18)

God is watching all our actions and words of kindness that we have for others. If our hearts and actions are unkind, the Holy Spirit of God can be grieved(Ephesians 4:30-32). The kind person is respected(Proverbs 19:22, Romans 12:10) and honored with great rewards(Genesis 40:6; Romans 28:7-10).

Q

What can we learn from the small child where the miracle of Feeding of the 5,000 originated? (John 6:9)

4) Embrace and forgive them.

Everyday we need forgiveness and we need to forgive others. The Lord's Prayer teaches us that we must pray for our daily bread, we must pray for a daily portion of forgiveness, a daily portion of spiritual strength so we do not fall into temptation or evil(Matthew 6:11-13).

God forgave us first, so we must forgive others(Matthew 18:21-35). Forgiveness is for myself above all else(Matthew 6:14-15). It is God's grace to be compassionate and forgive one another(Ephesians 4:32; Genesis 50:20).

Q

Among the famous works of Georges-Henri Rouault, A juniper tree leaves its scent on the ax that bears it. Think about the meaning of these words.

Blessed Be the Fountain of Blood

H. S. Perkins

Commitment and Application

1. What grace has God given you during this past week?

2. To this point, we have studied about having a "Positive View of Others." Let's share what we felt and realized today in our sharing time.

3. Share why slandering or gossiping about others is bad and what negative consequences it has.

4. Share any experience of receiving great comfort and strength from words of encouragement or praise.

5. Think about how you can develop what you're lacking in the four ways you can have a positive view of others.

Today's Assignment	Choose one of your family members or acquaintances and write something positive, encouraging, or praise them. Share with them.

Memory Verses

"Be kind and compassionate to one another,
forgiving each other,
Just as in Christ God forgave you."
Ephesians 4:32

Proclamation of Absolute Positivity

"I will honor others and love them.
I believe God will bless them through me"

Meditation Quote

"Write injuries in dust, benefits in marble."
Benjamin Franklin

POSITIVITY

The 4th Dimension
Absolute Positivity Training School

05

Fivefold Positivity ③: Positive View of Work and Calling

05 Fivefold Positivity ③: Positive View of Work and Calling

A boy lost his father at the age of 13 and lost his sight at the age of 14. Shocked by the news that her son went blind, his mother passed away shortly after, and even his eldest sister passed away due to overworking. The remaining three siblings were scattered and there was no hope before them. People have told him, "Blind men can only work as a medium or as a massage therapist." However, the young boy firmly believed in God even in desperate situations and overcame all difficulties through absolute hope given by God

With the vision that God has given him in mind, he graduated from Yonsei University and received a Ph.D. in education from the University of Pittsburgh. And he was appointed Chairman of the State Department's National Disability Committee in 2001 to oversee the policy of the disabled in the United States. This is the story of Dr. Young-woo Kang who is now in heaven.

Dr. Young-woo Kang says this about his life. "God has given me the weakness of blindness but through it God has blessed me with numerous opportunities to meet with great people, makes the world a better place." He says he was 'blessed through blindness' not 'disregarded because of blindness.' This is how he was able to enjoy all of his blessings.

Meditation

Even through my weakness, God's calling can be fulfilled (Judges 3:15; 2 Corinthians 12:7-9)
Meditate on weakness through God's calling in your life.

Positivity Quotient Check List ☑

Positive View of Work and Calling Quotient Check List?

Instructions: Please read each statement and select the most appropriate response to indicate how frequently you experience the behavior described in the statement.

Statements	Never	Rarely	Some times	Often	Always
	1	2	3	4	5
1. I am enjoying what I'm doing.					
2. I think the work I'm doing is God's mission.					
3. When faced with a difficulty, rather than giving up, I rise to the challenge.					
4. I often think of ideas while I'm working.					
5. I pray to God before I go to work and pray while I work.					
6. When I work, I am kind and considerate of the people around me.					
7. I work with passion.					
8. I do my best in everything I'm entrusted with.					
9. I don't think there is work or my mission has ended because I have aged.					
10. To get better at work, I manage my physical strength.					

After reading each statement, check the corresponding box.
Add up the checked scores for each statement.

Totals (   ) points

Encounter the Word

Read Ephesians 6:5-8.

5 Slaves, obey your earthly masters with respect and fear, and with
sincerity of heart, just as you would obey Christ. 6 Obey them not only
to win their favor when their eye is on you, but as slaves of Christ,
doing the will of God from your heart. 7 Serve wholeheartedly, as if
you were serving the Lord, not people, 8 because you know that the
Lord will reward each one for whatever good they do, whether they
are slave or free.

1. In what attitude should we work? (Verse 5)

2. What's the difference between pleasing people and pleasing God? (Verse 6)

3. For Christians, who do you serve and who is the final evaluator? (Verse7)

4. What is the ultimate reason why we should do our best in the workplace? (Verse 8)

5. According to the Bible, there are people who have been praised before God and people by working hard by doing their best with sincerity(Genesis 24; Genesis 39:21-23). Let's meditate on how we are.

Positive View of Work and Calling

People with positive self-perception tend to also be positive towards others and work with dignity. When we do our best where we're called faithfully, God will be with us in all we do and will bless us.

1. Importance of Positive View of Work and Calling

1) We give worship through our work

We must do all things as we do unto the Lord(Colossians 3:23). Because our work can also be worship unto the Lord. Robert Morray says, "Worship is all of life." Not only while you are at work, but while you're at home or anywhere and in whatever you do, you can worship the Lord(John 4:24).

2) God's calling can be accomplished through your work

It is said that there are four important encounters for a person. It is expressed as 4M. It is Master, God is the Master of my life, Mate, my partner in life, Mentor, a true teacher, and Mission, a mission in life. When we meet the God of absolute positivity, we discover our mission in life. Then we can live our purpose driven life.

3) In God, all work is holy

There are people who think that the world's work and God's work are separate but according to the Reformer Martin Luther from Germany, all jobs are a calling from God. Luther says,

"Through each of our jobs, we serve others and that is part of the worship that fill this world."

God created this world and he reigns through us(Genesis 1:28). We are to do our very best wherever and whatever we do with all our soul and mind, then it becomes our natural calling(Psalm 119:30). Through work, we may be blessed through it and enjoy happiness and success and give all glory to the Lord.

Q

When in Egypt Joseph served his master Potiphar and captain of the guards, as well as the cupbearer and baker in prison faithfully(Genesis 39:4; Genesis 39:21; Genesis 40:4). So, what happened because of his faithfulness? (Genesis 39:3-4; Genesis 39:23; Genesis 41:9-44)

2. Ways of positive perspective of our work.

1) You must have dignity in your work

Dignity in one's job means a calling and confidence in a job. Even if it's the same job, how I think about it changes my mindset about my job. When we have dignity as children of the king of kings, we will cherish our occupation as our calling and enjoy it(1 Peter 2:9).

Q

Who am I serving in my current work? (Colossians 3:23)

2) Do your best and be faithful even for the smallest things

The world's happiest person is someone who works full of joy, working and sweating, we reap what we have sown(Galatians 6:7). If we do not work hard day by day faithfully(Proverbs 6:8), we would not be able to receive God's blessings and grace. God is faithful so we must be faithful as well. The most precious time of our life is the present and we must eat of the faithfulness of the Lord as our food(Psalm 37:3).

Q What did the Apostle Paul share with the people in the church of Thessalonica about work? (1 Thessalonians 4:11)

3) Work with enthusiasm

Enthusiasm is the core DNA value of successful people. God is the God who works, He does not rest but works for the salvation of mankind. Jesus is at work as well, He did not spare his own life for us(John 5:17) God sent us the Holy Spirit(John 16:7), who is interceding for us(Romans 8:34; Hebrews 7:25) and is preparing a place for us in heaven(John 14:3). He is at work in charge of leading us all the way to salvation(Revelation 7:10). We follow after Jesus' enthusiasm and passion for us. Every day we must pray to receive the passion and power from Him.

Q Who is one of the most passionate disciple in the Scriptures and what are the reasons? Share your thoughts.

4) Keep your calling for a lifetime

Currently, a Korean's average life span is about 84 years old. We are to have the calling in our mind until the day we die. Abraham was called when he was 75 years old, Moses was called to lead the exodus in his 80s, Caleb conquered Hebron Mountain when he was 85 years old. Until your calling is over, your life isn't over yet. Until the day we stand before the Lord, we are to move forward towards the work of our Lord.

Q What do you think drove Caleb to be at work for God so passionately even when he was 85 years old? (Joshua 14:10-12)

O, Master, Let Me Walk with Thee

W.Gladden, H. P. Smith

Commitment and Application

1. What grace has God given you this past week. Let's share together.

2. To this point, we have studied 'Positive View of Work and Calling.' Let's share what we felt and realized today.

3. What do you think is the special talent and mission God has given you?

4. What vision or work inspires you to be passionate?

5. How old are you? How will you live the rest of your life now? Let's take time to make a decision and have a time of prayer.

Today's Assignment	Choose one of your family members or acquaintances and write something positive, encouraging, or praise them. Share with them.

Memory Verses

"Whatever you do,
work at it with all your heart, as working for the Lord,
not for human masters."

Colossians 3:23

Proclamation of Absolute Positivity

"I am grateful for the work and mission that
God has called me to.
I promise to follow through faithfully!"

Meditation Quote

"If you stick to the world's profession
with a holy heart, it is no longer worldly,
but part of life dedicated to God."

A. W. Tozer

POSITIVITY

06

Fivefold Positivity ④: Positive View of Environment

06 Fivefold Positivity ④: Positive View of Environment

In July 2000, a driver crashed into a car causing a 7-car collision. A student who was on her way home in her brother's car after studying in the library was also one of the victims of the accident. The 23-year-old student, who suffered third-degree burns over 55% of her whole body, was diagnosed with a first-degree facial and physical disability at the time. After the accident, dozens of surgeries and a lot of pain were waiting for her. However, Ji-son Lee looked at her life in positive way without grumblings or resentment towards her situations. She made it through day by day with her optimism.

After 23 years, she became a professor at Ewha Woman's University where she graduated from. She says, "As life changed completely after the accident, there was an entire change in my view of God. I realized that I was a cast member in a movie that God planned, and God wrote and directed the scenario."

God is the movie director of our lives. The joy, sadness, and every moment of life are combined to make it the best symphony. So don't panic or be afraid when you encounter a problem.

Meditation

There are times when you encounter unexpected difficulties in life.
Let's think about how we should accept it and deal with this situation.

Positivity Quotient Check List ☑

Positive View of Environment Quotient Check List?

Instructions: Please read each statement and select the most appropriate response to indicate how frequently you experience the behavior described in the statement.

Statements	Never	Rarely	Some times	Often	Always
	1	2	3	4	5
1. I don't complain when problems arise.					
2. I don't dwell on past wounds and torment myself.					
3. I believe everything that happens to me and my environment is in God's providence.					
4. I often remember the grace God gave me and gain strength.					
5. I believe God will work together for the good even in difficult situations.					
6. I tend to think positively about the community I belong to.					
7. I pray for and love the church I attend.					
8. I cherish and value my company.					
9. I don't criticize people in my community.					
10. I always have a positive attitude when I'm with or working with people.					

After reading each statement, check the corresponding box.
Add up the checked scores for each statement.

Totals (   ) points

Encounter the Word

Read Numbers 14:1-9.

> [1] *That night all the members of the community raised their voices and wept aloud.*··· [3] *Why is the Lord bringing us to this land only to let us fall by the sword? Our wives and children will be taken as plunder. Wouldn't it be better for us to go back to Egypt?* ··· [8] *If the Lord is pleased with us, he will lead us into that land, a land flowing with milk and honey, and will give it to us* [9] *Only do not rebel against the Lord. And do not be afraid of the people of the land, because we will devour them. Their protection is gone, but the Lord is with us. Do not be afraid of them."*

1. Why did the members of the community raise their voices and weep aloud all night long? (Verse 1; Numbers 13:31-33)

2. What misunderstanding did the Israelites have of the Lord? (Verse 3)

3. What confessions of faith did Joshua and Caleb have? (Verse 8)

4. With what faith did Joshua and Caleb urge the Israelites to have? (Verse 9)

5. What lesson can we learn from the faith of Joshua and Caleb?

Positive View of Environment

Our thoughts and actions are influenced by the environment. On the contrary, the attitude we have affects the environment. What matters more aren't the problems itself but our positive attitude towards the problems. Even when we confront difficulties in the community, we must overcome them together with the power of positive attitude. We must believe that our faithful God is over everything and He is in total control(1 Chronicles 29:11; Romans 8:28; Psalm 18:16).

1. Ways to overcome hardships

1) Forget the former and negative things of the past

People who can't get out of a problem or someone who causes a problem have a common characteristic. They constantly reflect on past mistakes, failures, and wounds in their mind. God tells us to clean up the past before we do anything new(Isaiah 43:18, 1 Peter 4:3). The past failures should be a mirror for the future, and the experiences of success should be used as a steppingstone for higher gains. When you get out of your past sins and wounds(Psalm 103:12), with a changed mind, you can overcome the problem and succeed with a new vision.

Q What negative past do you have to leave under the foot of the cross? (Galatians 2:20) Repent and pray at this time. Trust upon the blood of Jesus to forgive you and pledge to start anew.

2) Remember your spiritual landmark

It is important to remember the positive experiences of the past when you encounter a problem. Landmarks refer to symbolic place such as buildings, symbols, sculptures, etc. Just as Samuel defeated the Philistines and built the monument in Ebenezer, the journey of faith requires spiritual landmarks(1 Samuel 7:12). When David fought against Goliath, the Philistine, he went forward and proudly defeated him, remembering the help of Jehovah, who protected him from the jaws of the lion and the bear's claws(1 Samuel 17:34-36). In a negative situation, you have to remember the emotions when you first met the Lord, the prayers that were answered, and the moments of grace you received(cf. Revelation 2:4-5).

Q Let's reflect on some of the landmarks we should remember?

3) Experience breakthrough with positive prayer

Positive prayers are spiritual dynamites that break the power of negative environment and its powers(Jeremiah 29:12). When we are downtrodden and exhausted, we must remember that our Lord tirelessly cares for us and knows every detail of our lives. Continue to pray on(Psalm 102:17). We must come to the Lord with prayer of absolute positivity. Then He will answer us and show us mysteries that are unknown(Jeremiah 33:3). We must not fall into despair but pray, then we will see the miracles of God(Luke 18:1-8; Galatians 6:9).

Q Do you have prayers that need breakthrough? Let's read Jeremiah 33:3 and memorize the verse. Pray while you hold onto the verse.

2. Positive perspective towards our community

1) Positivity in community and team synergy

So, life is not a song that you sing alone at the top of your voice, but rather a symphony that listens to each other and creates harmony(cf. 1 Corinthians 12:12; Psalm 133:1). Therefore, you should look at the strength, not the weakness of the person next to you. Rather than the negative idea of "not because of him," you should have a positive idea of "I will succeed in combination with his strength."(cf. 2 Corinthians 1:19) When you have positive thoughts of your community, synergy will come and your community will experience growth(Ephesians 4:15-16).

Q Why are two or three better than one person? (Ecclesiastes 4:9-12)

2) Positive faith that builds the church

Some people search for "a church without any problems." But just as there are no life without a problem, there is no church without problems. There may be a lack of church communities, and there may be churches in difficult surroundings and conditions, it is important to look at the church in a positive manner, bless and build up the church. There should be no reckless criticism or hasty judgment(Luke 6:37). Just as Jesus loved the church and sacrificed Himself(Ephesians 5:25), we must love and bless our church and serve those who belong to the church(John 13:34), and fill it with an atmosphere of grace and blessing. Positive faith and words saves the church.

Q What are we to do if we say we love our church? Share your thoughts on what we can do.

3) Positivity that edifies your work and communities.

If employees didn't have a positive attitude towards the company, customers wouldn't be able to have a positive attitude towards the company. People with negative attitudes lose the opportunity to work hard or grow in an organization. I have to serve and work with a positive attitude in the church or community I belong to(cf. Proverbs 28:18). Then the God of absolute positivity will surely bless the positive people. He allows good things in our lives.

Q Let us pray together for our work space and community that we belong to.

Where There is No Path

Lyrics by Hong, Young-Gi
Music by Hong, Seung-Ki

Commitment and Application

1. Let's share what grace God has given you this past week.

2. To this point, we have studied 'positive View of Environment.' Let's share what we felt and realized today.

3. What are some past wounds that have tied me up? If there is, let's take time to trust in the blood of Jesus and pray to gain freedom.

4. Let's write down at least 10 things where God has given us grace in the past.

5. How am I serving the church that I am currently attending? If you are attending a church, be more passionate. If you're not attending one, let's take a moment to make a decision to serve.

Today's Assignment

Write down and declare that you'll overcome the difficult environment or problem that you're experiencing.

Memory Verses

"Only do not rebel against the LORD.
And do not be afraid of the people of the land,
because we will devour them.
Their protection is gone, but the LORD is with us.
Do not be afraid of them."

Numbers 14:9

Proclamation of Absolute Positivity

I believe God's sovereignty is present
in my current environment
and I am committed to generate influence
wherever I am!

Meditation Quote

"Whether you think you can, or think you can't
Either way you are right."

Henry Ford

07

Fivefold Positivity ⑤: Positive View of Future

07 Fivefold Positivity ⑤: Positive View of Future

Pastor Hyun-chul Cho of Orange Hill Presbyterian Church in the United States was diagnosed with cerebral palsy at the age of one. He had to live with pain because of cerebral palsy that twisted his whole body, and he even had to twist his whole body to say a word. Then he received Jesus when he was in middle school. After that, God's grace came, and while reading the Bible and praying, he became a positive person who filled his future with positive dreams. The words from 1:27 touched his heart saying, "You raise the weak and shame the strong."(1 Corinthians 1:27)

'God will use me. God will be honored through me. I'll be a pastor in the future. I be a revivalist as well as a pastor!' This dream came into his mind and began to grow. People around him including his parents said it would be impossible. But he put up an American map and prayed day and night with his hand on the map. And God answered his prayer that envisioned the future of positivity. After graduating from seminary in Korea, he went to Azusa Pacific University in the U.S. and got a master's degree. And now, he became the first pastor with cerebral palsy and is doing ministry in a Korean Church in America.

Meditation

Spiritual dreams refer to looking at a blessed future with faith in the word of God (Hebrews11:1). What kind of word am I holding onto and looking into the future?

Positivity Quotient Check List

Positive View of Future Quotient Check List?

Instructions: Please read each statement and select the most appropriate response to indicate how frequently you experience the behavior described in the statement.

Statements	Never	Rarely	Some times	Often	Always
	1	2	3	4	5
1. I believe that God has great expectations and plans for my life.					
2. I feel optimistic and hopeful about my future.					
3. I'm expecting God to give me a miracle in my life.					
4. When I pray in the Holy Spirit, I feel my holy desires will come true.					
5. The vision and dream that God gives me is passionately enflamed in my heart.					
6. When hardship comes my way, I persevere with the dream, the friend that God has given me.					
7. I always picture achieving my vision and my future.					
8. I write down my dream and pray specifically to achieve it.					
9. I am always studying and learning to achieve my dream.					
10. I am a missionary to fulfill God's dream and vision until I die.					

After reading each statement, check the corresponding box.
Add up the checked scores for each statement.

Totals (   ) points

Encounter the Word

Read Genesis 37:18-20, Psalm 105:17-19.

18 *But they saw him in the distance, and before he reached them, they*
plotted to kill him. 19 *"Here comes that dreamer!" they said to each*
other. 20 *"Come now, let's kill him and throw him into one of these*
cisterns and say that a ferocious animal devoured him. Then we'll see
what comes of his dreams."

17 *and he sent a man before them— Joseph, sold as a slave.* 18 *They*
bruised his feet with shackles, his neck was put in irons, 19 *till what he*
foretold came to pass, till the word of the LORD proved him true.

1. What did Joseph's brothers do to Joseph? (Genesis 37:19; Genesis 37:5)

2. Why were Joseph's brothers jealous of him and hate him? (Genesis 37:18; Genesis 37:2-5)

3. What does scripture say about the one behind Joseph being sold as a slave? (Psalm 105:17; cf. Isaiah 53:10) What was God's plan through the incident? (Genesis 45:7-8; Genesis 50:20)

4. In the process of God's dream being accomplished, there are trials and difficulties. What are the meanings of the sufferings? (Psalm 105:19)

5. In the end, Joseph's brothers witnessed that despite many hardships, Joseph's dreams came true(Genesis 37:20). What is God's dream for my life and what attitude should I have until it is accomplished?

Positive View of Future

A positive person not only has positive thoughts of the past and present but also the future. As we look towards the vision and dream that God gives us, may we continue on with faith of absolute positivity, for God will work according to our dream and faith(cf. Mark 10:46-52; Isaiah 37:5-6).

1. The importance of positive future perspective

1) God who dreams

God is also a dreamer. God had a dream of putting Abraham as the ancestor of faith, and to make Israel be a kingdom of priests and a holy people to Him(Exodus 19:6). He had a dream for Israel, as His people. But God's true dream was Jesus Christ. God had a dream of saving mankind through Jesus. His real dream was of Jesus. God dreamed of saving the mankind through Jesus, and that dream was accomplished at the cross(John 19:30). Because we serve a God who dreams, we must be people who dream holy dreams.

2) We are God's dream

Just as Jesus was God's dream, we are God's dream. As parents have anticipation towards their children, God's heart is full of dreams and expectations for us. He wants us to know Him(2 Peter 3:18), be more like Him(2 Peter 1:4-7), serve Him(Philippians 2:17), and share about Him(Acts 20:24).

3) God who blesses our future

When we entrust our positive future to the Lord, we get to know of God's heart, who wants to bless us. He doesn't take care of things as they come, but plans thoroughly ahead of time(Ephesians 1:11). God wants us to enjoy good health and that all may go well with us, even as our soul is getting along(3

John 1:2). He wants to give us a big hope of the future. "For I know the plans I have for you," declares the Lord, "plans to prosper you and not to harm you, plans to give you hope and a future."(Jeremiah 29:11)

Q Declare the following sentence aloud three times. "I am God's dream!"

2. Ways of a positive future perspective

1) Seek to be filled with the Holy Spirit with anticipation

First, we should look forward to our life and our future. We should pray to be filled with the Holy Spirit. If the Holy Spirit comes, He will have God's vision for us, regardless of age or environment. We will have a dream of living for the gospel and missions(Joel 2:28, Acts 1:8). When we pray with the Holy Spirit, God leads our lives by giving us holy desires in our hearts(Philippians 2:13). And through us he does wonders and miracles(Isaiah 43:19).

Q When there is no revelation or dreams from God, what would our lives be? (Proverbs 29:18) Let us continue to seek to know God's dreams with prayers in the Holy Spirit and the word of God.

2) Visualize your dreams and pray specifically

Before using His servants, God trained the chosen to dream in faith(Genesis 13:14-15; Genesis 15:5; Genesis 37:6-10). Visualization of your faith is important(Romans 4:20). To accomplish your dream, you must look to them with faith(Hebrews 11:20).

You should write down your dreams about individuals, families, churches, and visions related to work or business, and look at them and pray. The dream will come true when you set clear dreams and goals, pray specifically, and seek God's wisdom and ability(cf. Joshua 14:12; Isaiah 38:2-6; Jeremiah 33:2-3).

Q	Let's close our eyes for a moment and visualize our dream.

---

3) Remember that hardships and dreams are our friends

Suffering is a milestone in God's dream(Psalm 119:71). People of faith were used by God after they have gone through the tunnel of hardship. After 25 years Abraham received God's call(Genesis 21:2), for Joseph it took 13 years (Genesis 41:41), and Moses was trained in the wilderness for 40 years(Exodus 3:14) But at the end God's dreams were fulfilled.

Even though nothing is visible, nothing is audible, and nothing is held in your hand, when you persevere and believe in the God's word of promises, it will be fulfilled(Psalm 105:19; Psalm 119:67; 2 Corinthians 4:17).

Q	Try to reinterpret the sufferings you've experienced in God's sovereignty(Genesis 50:20).

---

4) Learn continuously

There is a quote "The Leader is a life-time learner."

We must continue to learn with a humble attitude(Matthew 11:29; 1 Timothy 4:15). There's a Latin word "Ancora Imparo." This is what Michelangelo Buonarroti, a genius artist said after he painted the famous painting, The Creation, at age 87 on the ceiling of the Sistine Chapel. We can learn from the people around us, and we can learn through our difficult conditions. You can learn through reading as well. Most of all, you must continue to learn and envision as you learn from the Holy Spirit who guides us.

Q Reading is important to achieve our dreams in the field we want(1 Timothy 4:13).

There's a Dream That I Dream

J.B.Pounds, C.H.Gabriel

Commitment and Application

1. Let's share what grace God has given us this past week.

2. To this point, we have studied 'Positive View of Future.' Let's share what we felt and realized today.

3. Why do I not have any expectations for the future and what should I do to have a dream?

4. Let's write down and share what we hope and pray for in the Holy Spirit every day this week(Philippians 2:13).

5. What am I thinking about and looking at the most right now? If there is an area of viewpoint that needs to be changed through today's learning, let's meditate on it and share.

Today's Assignment	Let's pray and write down with faith how our future self and God's dream will come true in the next 10 years.

Memory Verses

"For I know the plans I have for you,"
declares the LORD,
"plans to prosper you and not to harm you,
plans to give you hope and a future"
Jeremiah 29:11

Proclamation of Absolute Positivity

"I am the one who will fulfill
God's dreams and visions!"

Meditation Quote

"Visions and dreams are
the language of God the Holy Spirit."
Yong-gi Cho

08

Threefold Training ①: Proclamation of Positive Words

08 Threefold Training ①: Proclamation of Positive Words

There was a boy born in the slums of Detroit. The boy was ostracized by white students at school because of his black ethnicity. He was the last place in his class because he couldn't memorize the multiplication tables until he was in the 5th grade of elementary school. The boy later became the world's best doctor. He was the first person in the world to perform the separation surgery of Siamese twins. He became known as God's Hand, Dr. Ben Carson of Johns Hopkins University Hospital, Boleyn. He said that all, this came to be because of his mother's encouragements. She said to him,

"Ben, you can do anything if you want to. You can be anything if you try!" Her words of encouragement gave Ben Carson a hope and courage. This applies to us as well. We can give words of encouragement to others which will give hope and courage. We are to speak life into others' lives that give them hope and dreams.

Meditation

Let's take a good look at the words we use. Are they harsh on others? Or are they encouraging to others?

Positivity Quotient Check List

Proclamation of Positive Words Quotient Check List?

Instructions: Please read each statement and select the most appropriate response to indicate how frequently you experience the behavior described in the statement.

Statements	Never	Rarely	Some times	Often	Always
	1	2	3	4	5
1. Negative words never come out of my mouth.					
2. I often say words of encouragement and praise to others.					
3. I think positively of myself. I bless and declare.					
4. I believe that unbelief and negative words can distract from God's work and miracles.					
5. I often say words of blessings to others.					
6. I always read and meditate on God's Word.					
7. I pray by reciting the Word of God using it in appropriate situations.					
8. I give hope and words of life to others.					
9. I record God's vision and declare it whenever I have time.					
10. I believe there is power in words of faith. I declare and command diseases and problems to be healed and solved.					

After reading each statement, check the corresponding box.
Add up the checked scores for each statement.

Totals (   ) points

Encounter the Word

Read from 2 Kings 7:18-20.

18 *It happened as the man of God had said to the king: "About this*
time tomorrow, a seah of the finest flour will sell for a shekel and two
seahs of barley for a shekel at the gate of Samaria." 19 *The officer*
had said to the man of God, "Look, even if the LORD should open
the floodgates of the heavens, could this happen?" The man of God
had replied, "You will see it with your own eyes, but you will not eat
any of it!" 20 *And that is exactly what happened to him, for the people*
trampled him in the gateway, and he died.

1. The siege of the Aram army led to a severe famine in Samaria. What prediction did Elisha make at this time? (Verse 18)

2. How did the king's servant react to Elisha's prophecy? (Verse 19)

3. What happened to the officer who said words of unbelief and denial? (Verse 19-20; cf. Numbers 14:27-35; Luke 1:18-22; Isaiah 57:19)

4. Who should we listen to? (2 Kings 7:1; cf. 1 Samuel 17:28-32)

5. Elisha's prophecy came to fulfillment through the four lepers(2 Kings 7:3-16). What message does this teach us?

Proclamation of Positive Words

God created the world through His words, Genesis 1. Because humans were created in the image of God, we also have authority in language. Therefore, we should abandon negative words and speak life through positive and encouraging words that saves and blesses people around us.

1. Importance of positive language

1) Positive language affects all parts of our lives.

The tongue has the power of life and death, and those who love it will eat its fruit(Proverbs 18:21). There is also a saying, "A word pays off a thousand coins worth of debts." The faith of positivity gives birth to the language of positivity, and the language of positivity makes our lives positive. Positive words reveal positive power not only in our future but also in our interpersonal relationships(Proverbs 18:20).

2) Contagiousness of negative language

"The person bitten by a dog was treated and returned in half a day. The person bitten by a snake was treated and returned in three days. However, the person who was bitten by a person's word hasn't returned and is still hospitalized. This speaks about the powerful effects of the negative language(Psalm 140:3).

When the ten of spies returned from Canaan and gave negative reports, all of the Israelites were infected and cried in despair and blamed the leaders. Then God said, "As surely as I live, declares the Lord, I will do to you the very thing I heard you say"(Numbers 14:28). Negative thoughts give rise to negative words. Negative faith give rise to negative words, and negative words block God's miracle and darken our future(Mark 6:4-6; 1 Peters 3:10).

3) Words that save is important

Since the fall, mankind has destroyed the world and destroyed human relationships through constant negative words, words that kill. However, Jesus is a man whose words have become flesh(John 1:14). He healed and saved mankind(cf. John 11:43).

We too must speak life to save and heal people to resemble Jesus(Ephesians 4:29). "If anyone wants to speak, they should do so as one who speaks the very words of God."(1 Peters 4:11).

Q The Bible says what kind of word saves? (John 6:63)

2. Training methods of positive language

1) Your language changes when the Holy Spirit comes

Using the language of positive faith words isn't simply by human will or effort. We need the help of the Holy Spirit. "Being filled with the Holy Spirit" must be ongoing and present in our lives(Ephesians 5:18). We must desperately seek to be filled with the Holy Spirit.

Transformation of the words of our mouth and language is a crucial sign of someone who is filled with the Holy Spirit. When the Holy Spirit comes, our hearts are softened, we envision new dreams and prayer, praises and gratitude of our Lord will flow from our lips(Acts 10:46; Acts 19:6; Ephesians 5:19-20).

Q

Jesus' disciples were filled with the Holy Spirit and prayed in tongues as the Spirit led them(Acts 2:4,11). What is the spiritual meaning of tongues?

2) Engrave the words of the Lord in your heart

The Bible orders the word of God to be engraved on our hearts(Proverbs 7:1-3). As we do so when engraving on stones, the word of God will be engraved on our hardened hearts(Proverbs 3:3). The word of God revives people. We must always read the Word, meditate and memorize them(Habakkuk 2:2). We are to control all negative thoughts and words by using words of absolute positivity and words of faith.

Q

How did Jesus overcome the temptations of Satan? (Matthew 4:1-11; Deuteronomy 8:3; Deuteronomy 6:16; Deuteronomy 6:13)

3) Remember the power of Proclamation

Everything that exists in this world is governed by the power of what the people of faith say. Joshua ordered the sun to stop(Joshua 10:12) and Jesus also ordered the waves and the wind to be still(Mark 4:39). We too can pray and command our body, about the disease, about our situation and even about the future(3 John 1:2). For example, those who are ill, declare the promised words of healing(Isaiah 53:5), those who are anxious and worried should hold onto the words of peace(John 14:27; Philippians 4:6-7). We must declare in faith and pray continuously.

Q What are words of truth that I must hold onto and declare in faith?

____

____

4) Make a habit of proclaiming positive words

According to a paper published by researchers at Duke University in the United States, 40 percent of the choices we repeat every day are determined by habits, not by careful decision-making processes. The power of habit also affects our lives(cf. Jeremiah 22:21). We need to develop a habit for spiritual life(cf. Luke 22:39; Hebrews 10:25). Pray to be filled with the Holy Spirit(Acts 4:31), Read the Word and meditate(Deuteronomy 6:6), declare in faith(Psalm 107:22). These are some of the crucial habits to train ourselves that way miracles of absolute positivity will happen in our lives.

Q What are your morning routines? To experience "miracle mornings," what habits should we be trained with?

____

____

Wonderful Words of Life

P.P.Bliss

Commitment and Application

1. Let's share what grace God has given us this past week.

2. To this point, we learned about 'Training in the Proclamation of Positive Words.' Let's share what we felt and realized today.

3. Have you ever been tested with negative words or have been hurt by them? Let's share and pledge not to say negative words.

4. What do you think is the most important part of what you have studied today, for the training of positive language?

5. Let's write at least 5 Proclamations of positive language about our friend or the person next to you and encourage them.

Today's Assignment

Let's find at least 10 Bible verses related to the power and importance of positive language. Write them down, and recite them.

Memory Verses

"The tongue has the power of life and death,
and those who love it will eat its fruit."
Proverbs 18:21

Proclamation of Absolute Positivity

"I pledge to have a habit of positive language
by internalizing the word of God
with the power of positive words in mind!"

Meditation Quote

"Words, like flowers, have their colors too."
Ernest Rhys

POSITIVITY

09

Threefold Training ②: Absolute Gratitude

09 Threefold Training ②: Absolute Gratitude

There was a child born without arms and a right leg, except for his short left foot. His unusual appearance caused loneliness and despair, and during His school years, children ostracized and despised him. He thought of death from the age of eight, and at the age of 10, he actually attempted suicide but when he saw the news of someone who accidentally overcame a disability at the age of 13, he decided to do the following. "I'm going to choose between living in anger for the rest of my life because of what I don't have or be grateful for what I do have."

His life changed from that day on. The little boy, who had once contemplated suicide, later became an all-around sportsman who plays golf, enjoys surfing and horseback riding, and enjoys skateboarding. Reverend Nick Vujicic, a lecturer and best-selling author who is married to a woman he loves, gave birth to a child, travels around the world to deliver hope, and works as a representative of a mission organization for people with disabilities like himself.

This is what he says he. "How can I be happy without limbs? It's because I'm grateful for what I have without getting angry about what I didn't have right away."

Meditation How grateful am I for the things that I own?

Positivity Quotient Check List

Absolute Gratitude Quotient Check List?

Instructions: Please read each statement and select the most appropriate response to indicate how frequently you experience the behavior described in the statement.

Statements	Never	Rarely	Some times	Often	Always
	1	2	3	4	5
1. I confess my gratitude to God when I wake up in the morning.					
2. I look for something to be thankful for even the smallest things in my daily life.					
3. I often express my gratitude to people around me.					
4. I am grateful and pray even if there is no immediate response to my prayer.					
5. I confess my gratitude rather than my complaints even if something difficult happens.					
6. I don't complain about what I don't have, but rather, give thanks for what I do have.					
7. I meditate on God's grace by writing in my gratitude journal every day.					
8. I believe that hardships and problems are opportunities for faith and growth of character. I give thanks.					
9. I believe that God will make things for good even if things don't go the way I planned. I give thanks.					
10. I end each day with a prayer of thanksgiving before going to bed.					

After reading each statement, check the corresponding box.
Add up the checked scores for each statement.

Totals (   ) points

Encounter the Word

Read Acts 16:24-32.

24 When he received these orders, he put them in the inner cell and
fastened their feet in the stocks. 25 About midnight Paul and Silas were
praying and singing hymns to God, and the other prisoners were
listening to them. 26 Suddenly there was such a violent earthquake
that the foundations of the prison were shaken. At once all the prison
doors flew open, and everyone's chains came loose. 27 The jailer
woke up, and when he saw the prison doors open, he drew his sword
and was about to kill himself because he thought the prisoners had
escaped. 28 But Paul shouted, "Don't harm yourself! We are all here!"
29 The jailer called for lights, rushed in and fell trembling before Paul
and Silas. 30 He then brought them out and asked, "Sirs, what must I
do to be saved?" 31 They replied, "Believe in the Lord Jesus, and you
will be saved—you and your household." 32 Then they spoke the word
of the Lord to him and to all the others in his house.

1. What happened to Paul and Silas who followed the guidance of the Holy Spirit to Philippi, and how did they react to the situation? (Verse 24-25)

2. How did Paul and Silas' hymns and gratitude change the environment? (Verse 26)

3. What spiritual fruit did Paul and Silas' hymns and thanksgiving bear? (Verses 27-32)

4. There is a saying, "God is the God of the morning." What should I do when there's a dark night in my life? (Verse 25)

Training of Absolute Gratitude

If you believe in the God of absolute positivity, you can truly appreciate it in good situations as well as in bad situations. As we give thanks, faith in us towards our God of hope will rise. The confession of faith of absolute positivity and absolute gratitude are like two sides of a coin that cannot be separated. Therefore, the training of absolute gratitude is a really important factor in the life of the believer.

1. Importance of absolute gratitude

1) Absolute gratitude is the will of God

God commanded us to "give thanks always."(1 Thessalonians 5:18) God rejoices in those who come to Him with thanksgiving(Psalm 95:2; Psalm 100:4). He dwells in the heart of the meek and grateful. Gratitude is heavenly language(Ephesians 5:20). As the saying goes, "The language of division are words of complaint, resentment, and dispute, and the language of heaven are words of gratitude and praise." There should be no end to the confession of gratitude for the lips of the believer, the language of heaven(Colossians 4:2).

2) Absolute gratitude brings health and happiness

When you're thankful, a hormone called 'didorphin' is released, which makes you feel happy and healthy. Dr. Cathers Putt says there is a 'molecule of emotion' that conveys the emotions and thoughts of the mind to the body. The body and the mind are connected. So patients with chronic depression are more than four times likely to get sick, but people who give thanks can overcome stress and feel happy. As the saying goes, "Human beings are happy not because they are happy, but because they are grateful," they become healthy when they are thankful and happy when they are thankful.

3) Absolute gratitude brings miracles

We must give thanks in the name of Jesus in all matters(Colossians 3:17). When we give thanks, the miracle of salvation and the glory of God will be revealed(Psalm 50:23; Acts 16:24-32).

Before the miracle where Jesus fed the 5,000, He gave thanks in prayer and thousands ate until they were full(John 6:9-13). Before He raised Lazarus from the grave, He stood before the tomb and prayed, "Father, I thank you that you have heard me"(John 11:41-44), Lazarus came back to life. Gratitude is the seed of a miracle(2 Chronicles 20:20-22).

Q

How many times does Psalm 136 command us to be grateful? Also, what is the reason for gratitude and how many times do you give thanks?

2. Methods of absolute gratitude

1) Look at everything with positive eyes

Former Chairman Oh-hyun Kwon, who led Samsung Electronics' semiconductor said, "The word 'Yeok-kyung' meaning hardship contains the word 'reversal'. I interpret its meaning to reverse adversity when it comes our way. Adversity includes positive functions. We were given the opportunity to find out what the root of the problem is."

More than the circumstances, what matters is how you view the situation(cf. Numbers 13:30-33). If you look at it with negative eyes, you see only problems, however, if you look at it with positive eyes, you see opportunities. Therefore, you must thank God with absolute positive faith in any situation(Numbers 14:7-8).

> **Q** Why can we be grateful even in a situation of absolute despair? (Jeremiah 29:11; Psalm 136:1)

2) Let gratitude become a habit

Gratitude is a habit. You need to build upon it(Colossians 2:7). Jesus prayed according to His habit(Luke 22:39). Daniel never forgot to pray three times every day(Daniel 6:10). Giving thanks requires daily practice(1 Timothy 4:7; Luke 22:39-41). We must believe that God will work all things together for good even if the situation isn't good(Psalm 107:29-30). We must always give thanks. Keeping a journal entry of things that we are grateful for or a journal of gratitude are good ways to get into the habit of being grateful.

> **Q** Why did God teach Israel to observe the three Feasts(Passover, Pentecost, and the Feast of the Tabernacle)? (Exodus 23:14; Psalm 100:4-5)

3) Produce co-workers of gratitude

There is an African saying, "If you want to go fast, go alone, and if you want to go far, go together." Just as faith requires a fellow co-worker, a life of gratitude needs a partner(Ecclesiastes 4:9-12; Proverbs 18:24). Seek someone to be your gratitude partner(Proverbs 27:17; Proverbs 22:11). Share your prayer requests with your family, church, or at work as you pray together with people of faith(Psalm 133:1; Matthew 18:19-20).

Q Whose faith did Jesus see and heal the paralytic? (Mark 2:5)

4) Proclaim Thanksgiving daily

Words have power. What we say is projected into our body and mind. So our faith of absolute positivity must be declared in the language of absolute gratitude. When the Proclamation of faith is heard by our ears, our body, our heart, and our soul, we changes(Romans 10:10). When God's ears hear our confession of gratitude, God's power will be present in our lives(cf. Numbers 11:18; Numbers 14:28). Gratitude is the deepest confession of faith(Luke 17:11-19).

Q How does God introduce Himself in relation to the confession of our lips? (Isaiah 57:19)

Count Your Blessings

J.Oarman Jr., E.O.Excell

Commitment and Application

1. Let's share what grace God has given us this past week.

2. To this point, we learned about Training in Absolute Gratitude.' Let's share what we felt and realized today.

3. Share your experience of God's grace or miracle dealing with gratitude (cf. 1 Timothy 4:4).

4. There is a saying, "The gratitude of the past gives satisfaction to the heart, the present gratitude gives pleasure to the heart, and the gratitude for thc future makes the heart flutter." How do you feel now?

5. Which are of the Fivefold positivity requires more absolute gratitude? Positive view of self, others, work, environment, and future.

Today's Assignment Let's write down at least 15 things that we are thankful for.

Memory Verses

"Give thanks in all circumstances;
for this is God's will for you in Christ Jesus."
1 Thessalonians 5:18

Proclamation of Absolute Positivity

"I declare my gratitude to God every day
and in any situation!"

Meditation Quote

"Illness, poverty, and failure aren't God's curses.
If there is a curse from God,
then God is not believed,
Not being able to hear the word of God,
And you lose your gratitude."
Uchimura Kanzō

POSITIVITY

10

Threefold Training ③: Sharing Love

10 Threefold Training ③: Sharing Love

A deacon named Byung-rok Kim, a shoe repairman who has been repairing shoes since 1996, suddenly thought, "How many old shoes does each family leave unworn?" So he put a sign in front of his store, saying, "If there are shoes you don't wear or want to throw away shoes, please bring them to the shoe hospital." After that, about 5,000 pairs of shoes were collected, repaired, and distributed to neighbors in need. Deacon Kim's good deeds did not end here. He went to a nursing home to volunteer for haircuts and lived helping underprivileged children, boys and girls, and retired pastors. In addition, he sold 700 million KRW worth of land he bought with retirement funds in 2020 and donated it to those who have been struggling due to COVID-19.

Later, Deacon Kim said in an interview. "Christians like me have gained new life through Jesus, so the life they live is a bonus. So there's nothing to be greedy about. I'll give it all away before I go." Indeed, we are all living our lives as a bonus because of Jesus we have new life. Sharing love is the way to give back some of the grace our Lord has given to us as He has given us new life.

Meditation How am I implementing sharing the love in action?

Positivity Quotient Check List ☑

Sharing Love Quotient Check List?

Instructions: Please read each statement and select the most appropriate response to indicate how frequently you experience the behavior described in the statement.

Statements	Never	Rarely	Some times	Often	Always
	1	2	3	4	5
1. Knowing and sharing God's love is one of the core values of my life.					
2. I tend to look at the needs of the people I meet.					
3. If my neighbor or friend is in trouble, I am willing to help.					
4. I pray for family and friends who don't know the gospel.					
5. I use my gifts and talents to help the church and my neighbors.					
6. I preach the gospel to my neighbors and colleagues who don't believe in God.					
7. I participate in helping the poor in need.					
8. I pray for and comfort my neighbors who are ill or have problems.					
9. I share and help with programs in the church or community. I participate in campaigns such as blood drives, fundraising for relief, etc.					
10. I practice kindness and love without expecting anything in return.					

After reading each statement, check the corresponding box.
Add up the checked scores for each statement.

Totals (   ) points

Encounter the Word

Read Acts 9:36-40.

36 In Joppa there was a disciple named Tabitha (in Greek her name is
Dorcas); she was always doing good and helping the poor. 37 About
that time she became sick and died, and her body was washed and
placed in an upstairs room. 38 Lydda was near Joppa; so when the
disciples heard that Peter was in Lydda, they sent two men to him
and urged him, "Please come at once!" 39 Peter went with them, and
when he arrived he was taken upstairs to the room. All the widows
stood around him, crying and showing him the robes and other
clothing that Dorcas had made while she was still with them. 40 Peter
sent them all out of the room; then he got down on his knees and
prayed. Turning toward the dead woman, he said, "Tabitha, get up."
She opened her eyes, and seeing Peter she sat up.

1. As a female disciple of Jesus, what was Tabitha considered to be? (Verse 36)

2. When Tabitha died, who was invited? (Verse 38; cf. James 5:14-15)

3. What did Peter testify to those widows that gathered at the house of Tabitha? (Verse 39)

4. How did Peter pray for Tabitha? (Verse 40; cf. 1 Kings 17:21; John 11:43)

5. How was Tabitha coming back to life related to the life she lived? (Verse 36)

Training of Sharing Love

The clock in human history is divided into B.C. and A.D. B.C. stands for "Before Christ, Before Jesus Christ," and A.D. stands for "Anno Domini, the Year of the Lord." The timing is divided based on the birth of Jesus. I think there should be B.C. and A.D. in our lives, as well as in human history. Before knowing Jesus, we were different when we were under the power of sin and death, and after knowing. The transformation must show itself(Ephesians 5:8).

A person who has experienced God's love given through the cross, a symbol of absolute positivity, live to share the love received a with others around.

1. The importance of sharing love

1) Positive energy is recharged

A positive person can share love. A negative person can be transformed into a positive person if they practice love. Austrian psychologist, Dr. Alfred Adler, prescribed depression patients to "make their neighbors happy and give them love," and the patients who followed the prescription had experienced their depression being cured. Just like this if you share and give love, love and joy returns like a boomerang, and depression can be cured(John 12:24).

2) Sharing love is the key to the happiness

Hyung-seok Kim, an honorary professor at Yonsei University, known as the "philosopher over 100 years old," explains in an interview that selfish people can never be happy(2 Timothy 3:1-2). Love not only makes the one receiving it happy but also the one who is giving it(cf. John 3:16; 1 John 3:16). When we love, we go beyond ourselves and pass the state of being self-centered which is the root of all depression and anxieties. When we love and are loved, we become heathier and happier(cf. Proverbs 16:24; Hebrews 13:16).

3) It completes the highest calling of our life

At the cross of Calvary, through Jesus, all our negativities in our lives vanished(1 John 4:4). Through the faith of absolute positivity, from death to life, from darkness to light, absolute despair to absolute hope it has shifted(Colossians 1:13). Evangelizing and sharing love are our highest calling in life until we go see the Lord(Acts 20:24; John 13:34; 1 Corinthians 13:13).

Q

Think about and share whether you've ever felt joy in sharing love through doing small things for others(cf. Genesis 18:1-19).

2. Methods of sharing love

1) Bulk up your love muscles

Pastor Rick Warren says that we should practice and train the muscles of love often, just as we become strong and agile when we exercise regularly.

One of the trainings that God gave the people of Israel was the "training of giving." God first made the people of Israel offer the first fruit of all the crops(Exodus 23:19; Proverbs 3:9). The owners in harvest time did not harvest all the grain but left some ears of grain behind (Leviticus 19:9-10), taking care of the traveler or the widow(Deuteronomy 24:19-21). These are some of the trainings that God uses to bulk up our love muscles. Sharing and giving without expecting anything in return is the secret to be blessed greatly by the

Lord(Deuteronomy 14:29; Proverbs 19:17; Luke 6:38; Luke 14:12-14; 1 Timothy 4:8).

Q How does the Apostle Paul tell the elders of the church in Ephesus that he would be an example, who did he say are blessed? (Acts 20:35)

---

2) Share the good news of the gospel with prayer and love

The love of God who is absolutely positive and the life of Jesus is the good news of the gospel(John 3:16; Mark 10:45). Therefore, sharing the good news of the gospel is the highest form of sharing love with others. Although, preaching the gospel by shouting, "Believe in Jesus!" is necessary, we must continue to intercede and show love in action as well. When we love, people in the world will see the invisible God in us(1 John 4:8-11).

Q Who shared the good news of the gospel to you? (cf. 2 Timothy 1:5) Do you remember the moments how you were moved and overwhelmed?

---

3) Be attentive to the needs of others

To share love well, it is important to have sensitivity to people's needs. Jesus was not only sensitive to people's spiritual needs but was sensitive to their physical and emotional needs as well(Matthew 9:20-22; Matthew 14:15-21; John

4:14). Tabitha who was the member of the early church showed kindness by distributing handmade clothes to the poor(Acts 9:36-42). Sharing love begins from our small interest in the need of others.

Q What did Joseph see in the face of the cupbearer and baker? How did he interpret their dreams? (Genesis 40:5-19)

4) Life of sharing even the smallest things

Sharing love is not just about big and amazing things. The Apostle John said, "Anyone who has two shirts should share with the one who has none, and anyone who has food should do the same(Luke 3:11). We can share what we have; knowledge, and talents, and also by serving the church and the people who have the gifts of the Holy Spirit(Romans 12:6-8). Approaching someone to hear their stories and giving words of encouragement can also be a way of sharing love(Isaiah 40:1; Colossians 4:7-8). There is no better way, big or small in serving through love(Matthew 25:35-40).

Q Think of some small ways that you can share love(cf. James 2:15-17).

In One Fraternal Bond of Love

Shinsen Sambika c., D.B. Towner

Commitment and Application

1. Let's share the grace God has given to us this past week.

2. To this point, we studied 'Training of Sharing Love.' Share what you felt and realized during sharing time.

3. Love needs to be expressed(cf. Romans 5:8). Tolstoy said, "The most important person in the world is the person next to you," Say to the person next to you, "Bless you. I love you!" Let's confess to one another.

4. What did Jesus do as he knew His days on earth was ending? (John 13:1) How should we be living as our lives approaches closure? (cf. 1 Peters 4:7-8)

5. What are some of the things that I can do to share love?

Today's Assignment

Let's think about at least three ways to share love and practice it.

Memory Verses

"Give, and it will be given to you.
A good measure, pressed down,
Shaken together and running over,
will be poured into your lap.
For with the measure you use,
it will be measured to you."
Luke 6:38

Proclamation of Absolute Positivity

"I realize that God's love is
the most important mission in my life
and I pledge to share and love
even if in the smallest things!"

Meditation Quote

"A life lived for others,
is the only life worth living."
Albert Einstein

Proclamation of Absolute Positivity

1. I know the value and importance of absolute positivity and will devote myself to raising the positivity index!

2. I believe that God is the God of absolute positivity and trust God completely!

3. "I am the Lord's masterpiece and I believe that He will bless me and use me according to his will!

4. I respect and love others and believe that God will bless them through me!

5. I am grateful for the work and mission that God has called me to. I promise to follow through faithfully!

6. I believe God's sovereignty is present in my current environment and I am committed to generate influence wherever I am!

7. I am the one who will fulfill God's dreams and visions!

8. I pledge to have the habit of positive language by internalizing the word of God with the power of positive words in mind!

9. I declare my gratitude to God every day and in any situation!

10. I realize that God's love is the most important mission of my life and I pledge to share and love even in the smallest things!

Absolute Positivity Index(PQ)
Measurement and Evaluation

The Positivity Quotient(PQ) is the most important asset in life. PQ is a great force beyond IQ, environment, and destiny. The higher the PQ, the more amazing changes and miracles you'll experience in your life.

Welcome to the PQ Check List Evaluation after reading *The 4th Dimension Absolute Positivity Training School*. This is the time to measure and evaluate the Positive Index presented at the end of each chapter. Let's proceed in the following order.

1. Write down the Absolute Positivity Index scores of the 10 areas and add them up

* 50 points for each section. 500 points for 10 items.

No	Area	Total
1	Positive Attitude Quotient Check List	pts
2	Positive Faith Quotient Check List	pts
3	Positive View of Myself Quotient Check List	pts
4	Positive View of Others Quotient Check List	pts
5	Positive View of Work and Calling Quotient Check List	pts
6	Positive View of Environment Quotient Check List	pts
7	Positive View of Future Quotient Check List	pts
8	Proclamation of Positive Words Quotient Check List	pts
9	Absolute Gratitude Quotient Check List	pts
10	Sharing Love Quotient Check List	pts
Total		**pts**

2. Divide the total score by 5.(100pt conversion basis)

* **e.g.** | If your total score is 400, your score is 80 (400÷5=80).

Record your own score. (   ) pts

3. Find out your PQ (100pt conversion basis) level.

90~100pts	Your PQ level is Excellent. You are a very positive person.
	Having absolute positive energy, you can be happy and successful in whatever you do. Look forward to amazing miracles that will appear throughout your life.
80~89pts	Your PQ level is Above Average. You are a positive person.
	You have a high level of positive energy. If you use this energy, you can have great success. Make up for the shortcomings and move towards excellence.
60~79pts	Your PQ level is Average. You have a lot of positives.
	You have a lot of positive assets. Out of the 10 areas, which part were you most vulnerable? If you follow the guidance of the Holy Spirit, you can make up for the deficiencies. You can be the owner of absolute positive energy.
40~59pts	Your PQ level is Below Average. There's a fight between positivity & negativity in you.
	You need to take better care of your mind and thoughts. Please socialize with positive people and habituate absolute positive thoughts, Proclamations, and activities. There will be a big change.
39pts~below	Your PQ level is Low. Unfortunately, your negativity index is higher.
	A big effort is needed for the positive index but don't be disappointed. You have a God of absolute positivity. With intensive counseling and training, you can be a positive person, too.

The 4th Dimension
Absolute Positivity Training School

Published by CGW(Church Growth Worldwide)
CGW(Church Growth Worldwide) holds the exclusive publishing rights for both the Korean and English editions of this book.

- Address: 59, Eunhaeng-ro, Yeongdeungpo-gu, Seoul, Korea
- E-mail: icg7936@pastor21.net

Exclusive U.S. Distribution and Sales by LOGOS USA
LOGOS USA holds exclusive rights to distribute and sell this book in the U.S. publishing market. For any inquiries regarding purchases, please contact LOGOS USA.

- Address: 3268 Smithtown Road, Suwanee, GA 30024, USA
- E-mail: logosusainc@gmail.com
- Phone: +1 770-945-4447

ISBN 978-89-8304-365-8 (03230)